Poetry Workshop and Bible Study

A Biblical Study on Big Emotions
With a Practical Guide to Poetic Expression

by S. L. Mokry

Poetry Workshop and Bible Study and Big Emotions

All Text except Biblical Quotations- Copyright © 2025 by Shannon L. Mokry
Published by: Sillygeese Publishing, LLC

All Bible Quotations are NIV unless otherwise stated. Scripture quotations taken from The Holy Bible, New International Version® NIV®
Copyright © 1973, 1978, 1984, 2011 by Biblica, Inc.
Used with permission. All rights reserved worldwide.
All rights reserved.

For information or written permission for use of non-Bible portions of this work, please contact:
Sillygeese Publishing, LLC
P. O. Box 1434
Elgin, TX 78621
info@sillygeesepublishing.com

ISBN- 978-1-951521-62-2

CONTENTS

INTRODUCTION -1

WHY POETRY-3

HOW TO USE THIS BOOK - 5

POETRY FORMS-

- Haiku - 08
- Cinquain - 10
- Free Form - 12
- Blank Verse - 14
- Limerick - 16
- Clerihew - 18
- Triolet - 20
- Dizain - 22

BIG EMOTIONS - 24
BIBLE STUDY

- Anger - 26
- Depression - 34
- Anxiety - 42
- Sadness - 48
- Lonliness - 54
- Guilt - 64
- Joy - 72
- Happiness - 78

POEM WORKSHEETS- 86

Introduction

My name is Shannon L. Mokry, and I grew up in the church. I believe that it is not the name on the door that defines your Christianity, instead it is your faith and your desire to live the life of a Christian. Through that desire, you pursue knowledge and turn to the Bible for answers.

I don't have a fancy degree, but I have studied both early childhood development and English studies. I am also a homeschool mom that leads by example. I read a lot! I also write and have taught myself the ins and outs of being a small publishing house. After following God's directions for my life, I have published over twenty children's books. But God wasn't done with me there; after some more pushing, I have put together this poetry workshop and Bible study.

I had a hunch that this was where I was headed eight years ago when God pushed me to publish my first children's book. Our God is amazing, and when we let Him lead, the way and skill are prepared for us. He has a way of pushing us in the directions He created us for.

You can check out my blog for the full story behind my start in publishing, but for now I will say God is faithful and provides what is needed when it is needed.

God gave us the Bible. God gave us the Holy Spirit to help us understand. He also gave us teachers and elders. He directed us to mentor one another and hold each other accountable. He also gave each of us gifts.

If He has already given us so much, why am I writing this book? The Bible is huge, and it can be hard to both read and understand. Our Heavenly Father understands this and puts teaching into the hearts of some of His followers, like me.

I have the heart of both a teacher and a student. This book came to me from both my own experiences as a teenager and adult with Big Emotions and my vocation as a writer.

I do not claim to have all the answers, but through prayer, research, and the help of people who have made biblical study and/or biblical counseling their lives' work, I have created this book.

I hope you find it useful on your walk with the Lord.

I also encourage you to talk to your own spiritual advisor or counselor.

This book is not meant to offer medical or psychiatric advice.

Why Poetry

All types of writing have been proven to be beneficial to mental health and improving the overall skill of the writer. So why poetry? Poetry has a special place in the mix because it challenges the writer in ways that other types of writing does not.

It challenges the writer to expand their vocabulary and to shape their vision into a specific form. Poetry is not just beautiful; it can be funny, heart wrenching or joyful. Poetry challenges both the writer and the reader.

As you explore finding your writing voice, challenge yourself to try each type of poem more than once. You may find that certain styles call to you more, or that certain styles fit certain emotions better than others.

Poetry can be written while in the throes of Big Strong Feelings or clinically as a simple writing assignment. Try both and compare which one has the greater appeal—you may surprise yourself.

Are you still asking why poetry? Ask instead, why not?

Dive deeper. What is your goal? What do you hope to gain from this study?

_____

_____

S. L. MOKRY

How to Use This Book

This book is not intended to be read straight through, but rather to be gone through repeatedly, picking the emotions that call to you first, then tackling the harder ones as your skills and knowledge grow.

It is also intended to be a resource during those moments of strong emotion, to come back to over and over again, to help you find your way through them.

Document both your highs and lows so that you can go back to them and learn and grow in your ability to handle those emotions, your skill as a writer, and, most importantly, your faith and knowledge in how God moves in our lives.

Once you find that you have used up all the space provided, you can use a notebook, noting each poem with the emotion you are working through and the poem type you are attempting. I have created some journals to help in this process, but they are totally optional.

You may also find it helpful to notate additional Bible verses as you find them.

Example notations may look like this:

Poem poem poem
dream a little dream
poem poem poem
-Joyfulness, Free Writing

or

even my dreams are hopeful and inspiring.
06-01-20xx

or

-The book of John is calling to me today. Especially these verses... and list them.

Your thoughts?

_____
_____
_____
_____
_____
_____
_____
_____
_____
_____
_____
_____
_____
_____
_____

Poetry Forms

Poetry can be broken up into two main types: rhyming and non-rhyming. Within each type are several different forms. The rhyming forms are considered harder, but don't let that scare you. I suggest trying them all at least once—both as a personal challenge and an exploration in emotional release.

Non-Rhyming:

- Haiku
- Cinquain
- Free Form
- Blank Verse

Rhyming:

- Limerick
- Clerihew
- Triolet
- Dizain

This is not a complete list of poetry types, but the most commonly taught in the US. Feel free to play with additional forms if you are familiar with them or as you learn them.

Haiku

The haiku poem is a traditional Japanese poetry form consisting of three lines. Rhyming is not required, instead it is all about syllables, each line in the form having a set number of syllables for the language it is being written in. The form looks like this:

Example emotion: Happiness
Form: 5, 7, 5

>Oh beautiful sun
>Oh, bright and glorious day
>How much I love thee

Now you try...

_____

_____

_____

_____

_____

_____

5 _____

7 _____

5 _____

POETRY WORKSHOP AND BIBLE STUDY — HAIKU

5
7
5

5
7
5

5
7
5

5
7
5

Cinquain

The cinquain is similar to the haiku because it is short and powerful with just five lines and a set syllable count; it is an exercise in careful word choice. Here is the form:

Example emotion: Depression
Form: 2, 4, 6, 8, 2

> Dark night
> My heavy heart
> Lonely but not alone
> God does not forsake even me
> My God...

Now you try...

2
4
6
8
2

CINQUAIN

2
4
6
8
2

2
4
6
8
2

2
4
6
8
2

FREE FORM

Free form poetry is a unique form that does not adhere to any specific rules or conventions. It offers the writer more freedom to express themselves. That is part of what makes free form poetry so attractive and comparatively easy. It completely removes any limitation or confinement in terms of how the writer needs to express themselves. That doesn't mean it can't have structure, only that you set that structure following where your inspiration takes you.

This is my favorite, and the form I go to the most. For me, it allows for the free flow of thought without needing to worry about form.

Example emotion: Anxiety

>I breathe deeply
>It catches and I feel my lungs cry out.
>My heart races
>
>I might faint
>I might lose my breakfast
>I might...anything or nothing.
>
>I need something, something lost.
>Something important...
>Important to me...to me...
>
>I cannot move on
>Frantic, panic, manic, it is all the same.
>The struggle consumes all.
>
>Until...
>I fall to my knees in prayer...

POETRY WORKSHOP AND BIBLE STUDY   **FREE FORM**

Now you try...

Blank Verse

Blank Verse
All the emphasis is on meter and syllables. Each line must be ten syllables with no restriction on the number of lines or stanzas.

Example emotion: Sadness

> I feel my heart aching inside of me,
> Tears fall leaving trails that glint in the light,
> Words will not form in my mind or my lips,
> I am only half living in this fog,
> This painful ache that follows me always.
> I know it is grief, and it will not last,
> But sadness knows not time just this moment,
> A mere moment that stretches out and out...
> Then, only a memory, that lingers...

Now you try...

POETRY WORKSHOP AND BIBLE STUDY

BLANK VERSE

LIMERICK

Another short and popular form is the limerick. It consists of five lines—this time in rhyme. The limerick tells a story, and while often funny, that isn't a requirement. Here is the form:

Example emotion: Anger
Form: AABBA

> Hey Mister
> You drive like a mobster!
> Can you not tell one pedal from another?
> Or is your foot simply light as a feather?
> Even my grandmother drives faster!

Now you try...

A
A
B
B
A

POETRY WORKSHOP AND BIBLE STUDY — LIMERICK

_____
A _____
A _____
B _____
B _____
A _____

_____
_____
_____
_____
_____

A _____
A _____
B _____
B _____
A _____

_____
_____
_____
_____

A _____
A _____
B _____
B _____
A _____

CLERIHEW

The clerihew is similar to the limerick; it is also often funny, but is also often satirical. The rhyming form is AABB and can be one set or many. Be careful with this one as it must start with a person's name. Try a rhyming name or your own name, but not the name of someone you know as this form of poetry can lead to hurt feelings.

Example emotion: Maybe loneliness
Form: AABB

Tales of Burtle Turtle

On the subject of Burtle Turtle,
I must confess I feel sorry for his wife Myrtle.
Can you imagine Myrtle Turtle and her set of twins,
Triplets more like, with the tall tales he spins.

Oh, Burtle Turtle is quite the merry type.
At the end of the day they are all quite ripe!
Poor missus Turtle has gone quite nose blind.
Or for sweet smelling flowers she would have pined.

Now you try...

A
A
B
B

CLERIHEW

A
A
B
B

A
A
B
B

A
A
B
B

A
A
B
B

A
A
B
B

TRIOLET

The triolet is a French rhyming poem consisting of eight lines. There is a twist, though, for there are only five unique lines, with the first line being repeated as lines four and seven, and the second line being repeated as the last line. (I numbered my verses for purposes of an example, you can also number yours, just know that is not how it would normally be shared or read.)

Example emotion: JOY

Laughter

1. Laughter bubbles up and giggles spill out.
2. "Praise God" I shout.
3. I find I am blessed beyond count.
4. Laughter bubbles up and giggles spill out.
5. I am happy today, there is no doubt.
6. Happiness such as this, is a gift to the devout.
7. Laughter bubbles up and giggles spill out.
8. "Praise God" I shout.

Now you try...

_____
_____
_____
_____
_____
_____
_____
_____

TRIOLET

1. _____
2. _____
3. _____
4. _____
5. _____
6. _____
7. _____
8. _____

1. _____
2. _____
3. _____
4. _____
5. _____
6. _____
7. _____
8. _____

1. _____
2. _____
3. _____
4. _____
5. _____
6. _____
7. _____
8. _____

DIZAIN

The dizain is another traditional French rhyming poem, this time consisting of ten lines of ten syllables each. Yup, that is one hundred syllables total. (Once again I am numbering for example purposes.) The rhyming form looks like this:

Ex. emotion: Guilt
Form: ABABBCCDCD

Unloveable
1. I lay awake at night counting the stars.
2. I wish I could live in the countryside
3. It could not be worse than life without cars.
4. The life I live now I cannot abide.
5. Giving up everything left you bug-eyed.
6. My life is so sterile and I'm unloved.
7. It's no more than I deserve from my beloved
8. Still, sleep evades me every single night.
9. I lost every person I ever loved.
10. Redeem me, I don't wish to be a blight.

Now you try...

A
B
A
B
B
C
C
D
C
D

A
B
A
B
B
C
C
D
C
D

Big Emotions

God gave us these big emotions, but sin and the resulting separation from God often leaves us wondering why and how to deal with them. The good news is that God is good and gave us lots of examples to help us figure it out.

Here is a list of the emotions we are going to research and explore from a biblical view.

- Anger
- Depression
- Anxiety
- Sadness
- Loneliness
- Guilt
- Joy
- Happiness

- _____
- _____
- _____
- _____
- _____
- _____
- _____

This is not a complete list of emotions that you might be struggling with, so I included a place to list more.

Don't worry if you don't have any new emotions to add to the list, just know it is there for you if/when you need it. It is also good to note that many of these might be going on at the same time! Feel free to name these combos as a way to work through them.

As we go along, there will be plenty of space to take notes and explore your own findings.

My prayer for you is that you will develop the skills you need to grow in your faith and find the tools that work for you that accomplish self-control while feeling all the feels.

What is your prayer as you dive in?

_____
_____
_____
_____
_____
_____
_____
_____
_____
_____
_____
_____
_____
_____
_____
_____
_____
_____
_____
_____
_____

Anger

Bible Verse: Ephesians 4:26-27 NIV

"In your anger do not sin: Do not let the sun go down while you are still angry, and do not give the devil a foothold."

What Does This Mean?

I see this one misapplied or used to gaslight someone who is angry so often in our society. I want to break it down with you...

1. Anger is not sin.

2. Holding onto anger gives the devil a foothold, and this can lead to sin.

3. This does not mean forgive and forget. We are told to forgive as we are forgiven. God erases our sins—this is true. God does NOT erase our worldly consequences. In practical terms this means it is okay to protect yourself from future harm and the harm of others. Letting go of the anger and forgiving means not seeking punishment as a form of revenge. Holding someone accountable is NOT the same thing.

4. If it takes you time to cool off, then take that time, just be wary of holding onto it or feeding the anger. Holding onto anger can be the first step toward hate, and hate feeds anger. Hate is the opposite of love.

5. Cultivate tools to help you forgive and move on.
Ex: breathing techniques, physical or mental distractions

like writing poetry, or deliberately choosing to think of other things if your thoughts turn negative or dark.

Note: It is important with strong emotions, like anger, to take a moment and feel them, examine them, then choose to let them go and move on to more positive things.

Break it down further:

→ Who is this scripture written to?

→ What problems were they facing?

→ How does this apply today when held to the above answers?

Your thoughts...what do you need to be the person God created you to be?

Now, grab a pencil and your Bible.

*NOTE-Bible studies are most effective when you check your Bible directly.

Bible Verse: Proverbs 15:18 NIV

"A hot-tempered person stirs up conflict, but the one who is patient calms a quarrel."

What Does This Mean?

Letting your emotions rule leads to words that can't be taken back and actions that cause regret, harm, and long-term consequences. This is a verse about self-control as much as it is about anger. You can choose how you respond to external things. Choosing to not be offended and choosing to let slights go can take practice. Remember that all those things that trigger your anger response are minor compared to the damage of letting your anger rule your responses.

My breakdown on anger from the previous verse continues to hold true, but here is an additional breakdown for the reminder of what it means to be slow to anger.

1. In a crowd or gathering, people often look around to others to see how they should respond to divisive or insulting comments.

   Being calm and not reacting with anger or negativity can keep a situation from spiraling out of control.

   This is a reminder that self control is important.

2. In private moments, a misspoken word or misunderstood comment can create division. Allowing anger to be the default response causes relationships to break apart, become toxic, or worse.

You can't control how someone else chooses to behave, only your own actions.

Being slow to anger allows for conversation, understanding, and healing, and prevents further pain.

Additional verses or your thoughts...

Example: How does this verse make you feel?

_____
_____
_____
_____
_____
_____
_____
_____
_____
_____
_____
_____
_____
_____
_____
_____
_____
_____

Bible Verse: Matthew 21:12 NIV

"Jesus entered the temple courts and drove out all who were buying and selling there. He overturned the tables of the money changers and the benches of those selling doves."

What Does This Mean?

Jesus gives us an example of righteous anger. Those that had turned God's house into a place of commerce weren't there for the first time. This wasn't a first offense. Those in a position to stop it were turning a blind eye at best. He took radical action with no concern for who He angered in return.

You are not God, and you are not perfect. Be mindful of allowing your anger to overrule your concern for consequences.

God had a purpose for Jesus' actions. It was a step that was needed to send Him to the cross on the day and time He was sent.

Be always prayerful that your actions can point others to God. Who is in control of your anger? Who benefits from a display of anger?

Additional verses or your thoughts...

Example: How does this verse make you feel?

_____

_____

_____

POETIC WRITING WORKSHOP ANGER

POETIC WRITING WORKSHOP   ANGER

Depression

Bible Verse: Philippians 4:8 NIV

"Finally, brothers and sisters, whatever is true, whatever is noble, whatever is right, whatever is pure, whatever is lovely, whatever is admirable—if anything is excellent or praiseworthy—think about such things."

What Does This Mean?

What we think about and what we dwell on directly impacts our emotions. Really think about this. If you dwell on anger, what happens? You get more angry. If you dwell on that chocolate you're not allowed to have, all you want is that chocolate. This is also true with some forms of depression (to be clear, not all depression is the same). If you dwell on the negative, then you will continue to feel helpless and hopeless.

This verse is used by well meaning Christians and the world to cause shame and to leave us feeling unworthy and incapable. Let me reassure you that any use of God's word that leaves you feeling heavy laden is spiritual warfare. It is hard to remember when you are suffering from spiritual warfare that God is a God of peace and love.

Please, seek help with this if your thoughts turn to self harm or aggression of any kind.

In theme with this book, it is often helpful to put your thoughts and struggles into words. I'll list them here. Try one or both and see how they affect you.

1. This whopper of an emotion can have many causes. To start, focus on what is causing you to feel low. Is it exhaustion? The loss of someone or the loss of a relationship? Is it feeling unworthy of something? Take notes and pick a poetic style and focus on working it out and really identifying the cause.

2. Pick a style that doesn't fit with your emotion and twist the narrative to show the what ifs in a positive light. This may feel inappropriate if you are feeling depressed over a fresh loss, but only you can judge where you are in grief. It can also be super helpful if your depression is caused by negative self talk or the loss of a toxic relationship.

Additional verses or your thoughts...

Example: How does this verse make you feel?

_____
_____
_____
_____
_____
_____
_____
_____
_____
_____

Bible Verse: 2 Corinthians 1:3-4 NIV

"Praise be to the God and Father of our Lord Jesus Christ, the Father of compassion and the God of all comfort, who comforts us in all our troubles, so that we can comfort those in any trouble with the comfort we ourselves receive from God."

What Does This Mean?

This is a reminder that we are not alone! Depression is often coupled with isolation, so God wants us to know that we are never alone—He is with us, and He feels our pain and our suffering. He even sent His son to experience it firsthand. Notice also the second half of the verse, "so that we can comfort those in any trouble." One way God provides comfort is to put people in our lives that can help us.

That reminder is so important because the simple reminder that:

1. We are not alone.

2. Other people struggle with these same issues.

3. It is okay to seek help.

Depression is a complex issue, and it is different for each person experiencing it. God knew that when He knitted each of us together. That is why there is no one straightforward answer to this big emotion, but there are many tools to try out until you find the thing or the combination of things that helps you through it.

It is my prayer that this book and these carefully chosen verses will be one tool in your toolbox for better mental health and a better understanding of what God has to say. Prayer is another such tool. Use any of the spaces in this book to write out your prayers or speak your prayers into the notes of your phone. God wants that relationship with you.

Additional verses or your thoughts...

Example: How does this verse make you feel?

Bible Verse: Psalms 42:11 NIV

"Why, my soul, are you downcast?
Why so disturbed within me?
Put your hope in God,
for I will yet praise him,
my Savior and my God."

What Does This Mean?

First, I'd like to point out that psalms are poetry and songs written by David. In them we see David going through all the emotions we ourselves struggle with. Depression is no exception, and yet what does David ultimately do in these psalms? He turns the narrative from dark to light. No matter how dark and how inescapable life seems, offering up praise is the only thing to do.

Remember my previous note under Phillipians 4:8? David flips the script; he doesn't allow the darkness within to overcome him. He writes to God of hope and praise.

Whatever your choice before was, take a moment to pick an uplifting poetry style and write with a focus and hope for the future.

If you cannot see hope or improvement then PLEASE seek a counselor or trusted person (an adult if you are a teen), God has provided many resources, so let's use them.

Additional verses or your thoughts...

Example: How does this verse make you feel?

Anxiety

When I searched this term, many of the same verses came up that have been used almost as a weapon against those that suffer from anxiety as if we do not wish to rid ourselves of this burden. Instead, I wish to ask that you remember that God is not casting judgment on you. Through His son, your sins and your anxiety have been forgiven.

God's intention in providing the Bible for us is to provide comfort in this difficult world.
That is my prayer for you as you go through these passages...that you find comfort in them.

Bible Verse: Joshua 1:9 NIV
"Have I not commanded you? Be strong and courageous. Do not be afraid; do not be discouraged, for the Lord your God will be with you wherever you go."

What Does This Mean?

It means that God knows that the world is a hard place to live. Did He not come down in the form of Jesus and experience it with us? He knows...and still He tells us to let go of our fear. Be strong and courageous for He is with us. Meditate on that for a minute. Set this book down and just breathe deeply and think of God being with you.

The Bible is full of people (not characters, real people that lived and breathed just like you) that faced hard things. They did it not because they were better than you, or stronger than you, or even more gifted than you. They did it because they trusted God to be by their side through it all.

Now when you write your thoughts on this one, think about your anxiety from the perspective of the best outcome. How will you feel then?

Additional verses or your thoughts...

Example: How does this verse make you feel?

___
___
___
___
___
___
___
___
___
___
___
___
___
___
___
___

Bible Verse: Isaiah 41:10 NIV

"So do not fear, for I am with you;
   do not be dismayed, for I am your God.
I will strengthen you and help you;
   I will uphold you with my righteous right hand."

What Does This Mean?

We often see the Bible through one of two lenses. Who was the verse written too, and what does it mean to Christians today?

The third lens is what does it mean to me, personally? Can we get to that through the other two perspectives? Yes and no.

We may not always know what this verse or that verse meant to those it was written directly too. We might only know what it means personally.

Every person given as an example to us went through a season of this. Hold tight and cast out the anxious thoughts; they do not belong to you.

Additional verses or your thoughts...

Example: How does this verse make you feel?

_____
_____
_____
_____

Bible Verse: Matthew 6:27 NIV

"Can any one of you by worrying add a single hour to your life?"

What Does This Mean?

Just before writing this portion of this study, I spent an hour tearing up my house looking for a lost object. My heart was racing, and I felt faint and sick to my stomach. My anxiety about my lost thing was so high that I was in a state of panic over it. Now I have to go home and put my house to rights.

Not only did I lose an hour looking for a lost thing, but I'll probably spend another hour putting everything back in its place. The worst part? I didn't find it. I'm sure I will, probably when I don't have time for it. But if I don't? A week from now, a year from now? It won't matter.

So what does this verse mean? It means to put your trouble into perspective. Will this thing I am anxious over mean anything? Will it make any difference if I am anxious? I'm betting that no, being anxious won't improve anything, but letting it go will allow you to live your best life.

Additional verses or your thoughts...

Example: How does this verse make you feel?

_____
_____
_____
_____

Sadness

Why does sadness get its own category? Isn't it the same as depression? No it's not.

Depression is typically more severe, lasts longer, and has deeper core problems at play. Don't get me wrong, sadness can feel intense, but it is generally shorter lived and has a single focus. It can be anything from, "I'm sad that I missed the birthday party everyone else went too," or "I miss my dog; he was always with me, and now he is gone" (I know this one sounds deep, and it bears watching because it can lead to depression). Sadness can be an element of grief, but can exist on its own.

God did not create sadness as a way of punishing us. The Bible tells us that we are created for joy, love, and peace, but that God can use all things for our greater good. I believe that is the case with sadness as well.

Points to remember:
1. Sadness can stem from many things but is characterized by a feeling of loss or missing out on something. For some people, it is simply the opposite of feeling happy.

2. Sadness should not feel like it will never end. If you feel like you have always felt this way and will always feel this way, or your sadness lasts for more than a week or two, consider getting help.

3. If you have a history of extended sadness or depression, don't wait. Get help. Biblical study and expressive tools like writing poetry can help, but they should be used alongside professional help.

4. God can use sadness to your good.

Bible Verse: Matthew 11:28 NIV

"Come to me, all you who are weary and burdened, and I will give you rest."

What Does This Mean?

We are not meant to walk this life alone. God is with us through all the emotions, including sadness. God gives us hope for a better future and for eternity.

Additional verses or your thoughts...

Example: How does this verse make you feel?

_____
_____
_____
_____
_____
_____
_____
_____
_____

Bible Verse: Psalms 34:17-18 NIV

"The righteous cry out, and the Lord hears them;
    he delivers them from all their troubles.
The Lord is close to the brokenhearted
    and saves those who are crushed in spirit."

What Does This Mean?

Praying and talking with God shines a light on the way out of sadness. He walks with us, carries us, and never leaves us. God wants us to have a relationship with Him. The way to a relationship is communication. Take it all to Him in prayer.

Additional verses or your thoughts...

Example: How does this verse make you feel?

_____
_____
_____
_____
_____
_____
_____
_____
_____
_____
_____

POETIC WRITING WORKSHOP   SADNESS

Bible Verse: Matthew 5:4 NIV
"Blessed are those who mourn, for they will be comforted."

What Does This Mean?

Praying and talking with God shines a light on the way out of As I spoke of before, sadness can have its roots in grief or mourning. God wants us to give our grief and sadness to Him. To speak of it with Him and with each other. Do not hold your sadness close to your heart, instead talk about it and find comfort in that.

You are only alone if you choose to hold it separate.

Additional verses or your thoughts...

Example: How does this verse make you feel?

_____

_____

_____

_____

_____

_____

_____

_____

_____

_____

SADNESS

Loneliness

Many people think of depression when loneliness is mentioned or felt, but it is so much more than that. God starts the Bible with an understanding that man was not meant to live alone. That is why He created woman; people need companionship. That is not just being surrounded by other people, but a deeper connection with someone outside of themselves.

Loneliness is a feeling of missing out on that connection with others. It can include feelings of depression, or more accurately depression can lead to feelings of loneliness. Loneliness is listed separately because the two emotions can exist without each other. For example, one can be depressed but not feel lonely, and one can be lonely without being particularly depressed. The same is also true about sadness.

The world tells us that only sad and depressed people are lonely, but that is not true at all.
Loneliness can happen while you're otherwise happy and content. It is just missing a deeper connection with another person. Loneliness isn't one thing for everyone; it can be an element of other things. You are a unique person, and it's okay if several emotions become intertwined. It is equally okay if they stand alone and don't look like what you have seen in other people.

You might find that you are surrounded by friends or are otherwise happy or joyful but still have a nagging sense of missing something. If your loneliness is missing out on a deeper connection, then explore that, look into ways to change it, pray about the situation, and see what God brings to you. If you're feeling more than this, flip over to depression and sadness and know that it is okay to reach out for help. Deciphering our emotions and finding a healthy personal understanding isn't always easy, but it is worth the effort.

Now let's dive deeper into some Bible verses.

Bible Verse: Galatians 6:2 NIV

"Carry each other's burdens, and in this way you will fulfill the law of Christ."

What Does This Mean?

This verse was written by Paul not just for the new Christians in Galatia but to us as well. God knew what verses we would have today, and He knew what people then and now needed to hear. Like all verses, it is better read and understood with the rest of the chapter it was written with and who and what it was written for.

First, the misunderstandings around this verse. Paul was a lawyer and saw writings and teachings as such present things as law. In this fragment of what was written, it looks like we are responsible for our brothers' and sisters' and neighbors' burdens. That would seem to include financial and sinful struggles. That is not actually what is being said here.

If you read the rest of the chapter you would see that we are responsible for having a relationship with each other. To care and to communicate God's truth gently with one another so that no one feels they are walking this life alone.

We are told that we should be responsible for ourselves, but also be willing to help those around us. Likewise, we should be willing to hear and accept help when we need it. That is what relationships do and why they are needed, but we should also be careful that those friendships do not lead us into sinful ways ourselves.

Takeaway: Our need for connection with others can be an issue if that need leads us down sinful paths. The good news is that we are meant to be in fellowship with each other and help one another, so if you are struggling, reaching out to a fellow believer helps you both. It is part of God's design for us.

Additional verses or your thoughts...

Example: How does this verse make you feel?

___
___
___
___
___
___
___
___
___

POETIC WRITING WORKSHOP   LONELINESS

Bible Verse: 1 John 4:13 NIV

"By this we know that we abide in him and he in us, because he has given us of his Spirit."

What Does This Mean?

This was written by the apostle John to encourage us. Taken as a part of the whole chapter, it is a reminder that not everything that looks like it comes from God does. But there is good news! We are not left to figure out what is from God and what is against him on our own. We have been given the Spirit as a gift to help us figure these things out.

How this verse is often misrepresented is that you are not alone and, therefore, should not feel loneliness. For how could you be lonely if the spirit of God lives in you? Wow, right? What a way to not encourage someone. This is an example of someone looking like they are from God, but not doing God's work of encouraging you.

The truth of this verse is one of encouragement. God is with us, and He knows what we need. Because of this, He gave us the Holy Spirit to help us see the truth in others around us. This does not mean that we have no other social needs. In fact, we are told in Hebrews 10:25
 to not forsake the assembly of our brothers because God knows we need each other; we were created to be with others.

Additional verses or your thoughts...

Example: How does this verse make you feel?

POETIC WRITING WORKSHOP

LONELINESS

Bible Verse: Genesis 2:18

"The Lord God said, "It is not good for the man to be alone. I will make a helper suitable for him."

What Does This Mean?

This is the first thing at the beginning of the Bible that tells us that God made us for deeper connections. If you are not in a romantic relationship, this may be a feeling of longing for such. God created this in you, so be prayerful and mindful of it. If you are in a romantic relationship and still feel this sense of loneliness, consider if you are in a biblically sound relationship. The intimacy that you may be longing for was meant for marriage. It is not just a physical closeness, but an emotional one. Be careful where you give your heart and your body, but God has created this need in you, so He will also provide the partner that you need.

Focus on communication skills to deepen all relationships—those between yourself and God, yourself and friends, and from that trust that God will lead you to people or the person that will help in your needs.

It is also good to note that not everyone feels a need or draw toward romantic relationships, and that is okay too. Do not let anyone pressure you into a relationship on any level. This is written to help you think about where your loneliness may be stemming from, not to pressure you into something that you feel no call toward (see versus like Matt. 19:10-12).

Additional verses or your thoughts...

Example: How does this verse make you feel?

POETIC WRITING WORKSHOP　　　　　　　　　　　LONELINESS

Guilt

What is guilt and why do we feel it? What purpose does it serve? Those are good questions, and important questions, to understand because guilt is often the biggest hurdle between a person believing in God, believing in Jesus, and making the next step in giving over their life to Him.

Guilt is often depicted as a little voice on your shoulder telling you when you are doing something wrong then making you feel about it. You might even hear Christians say things like it's the Holy Spirit leading you to repent, or that it is God's way to punish you so that you won't commit that sin again. I assure you God is smarter than that, and He doesn't want to manipulate you that way.

To put it simply, guilt is what happens when you know you did something wrong and you are struggling to forgive yourself. Those that never feel guilt do not see themselves as doing wrong; they see the world through a self-centered lens. Learning to forgive is not the same as not feeling guilty, just as a misguided sense of guilt; it is not the same as not feeling guilt at all.

Let me give two examples:

1. A person sticks their foot out to deliberately trip another person. It works and everyone but the fallen person laughs. Did that person do wrong by deliberately tripping someone? YES! Feeling guilt shows an ability to feel empathy; not feeling guilt means that person does not feel empathy. Does it mean the tripper is a bad person? Not necessarily—we all

mature at different rates and paces. If that is you, take this time to really consider how the other person, the one that fell, felt. Take time in the future to mentally put yourself in the position of being hurt. Self awareness is great, and empathy is also important.

2. You see someone stick out their foot, knowing that it will trip your friend, and you say nothing. Maybe you even laugh with everyone else. Immediately, or sometime later, you feel guilty about not saying something, but mostly you are just relieved that the attention was not on you. Did you do the wrong thing? Yes, even if the motive was self preservation. This guilt is called empathy; it shows you are able to see outside of yourself.

The purpose of guilt is to teach us empathy. Without empathy, we cannot understand the gift of the crucifixion, we cannot see our own sins and repent from them, and we cannot understand the nuances of right and wrong. Instead we justify our actions and live as if no one and nothing else matters. We have no need of God or His sacrifice. Guilt shows us the path to mercy and forgiveness, not just for ourselves but for others around us as well.

If you are holding on tightly to guilt over something, I urge you to take it to God in prayer and look for a path to forgiving yourself. Know that if you are a Christian then Jesus has already paid for that sin, and you no longer need to hold onto it. Just as God wants you to forgive others, as He has forgiven you, He also wants you to forgive yourself.

Bible Verse: 1 John 1:9 NIV

"If we confess our sins, he is faithful and just and will forgive us our sins and purify us from all unrighteousness."

What Does This Mean?

This one is pretty straightforward. Some people might give you a list of things you need to do to be forgiven, but all God wants is a relationship. Ask with a true desire for forgiveness and He will erase it as if it never happened. This is not the same as doing whatever you want because God has forgiven you. God knows your heart, so if you have a heart for Him, a heart of love and peace, and a desire for a relationship with Him, He knows it.

There is no room in faith for legalism, only a relationship.

John was talking to first-generation Christians, and all the religions around them had strict rules and separation between God (or gods) and His (or their) people (Christians then, just as now, came from a wide variety of religious backgrounds). So this verse was written to show us that we don't have to pay a fee, sacrifice something, or beg for the ear of someone more holy than ourselves. Have faith, confess, and He will forgive.

Additional verses or your thoughts...

Example: How does this verse make you feel?

___
___
___
___

Bible Verse: Romans 8:1 NIV

"There is therefore now no condemnation for those who are in Christ Jesus,"

What Does This Mean?

This is the Good News! No longer are we held captive by our sins, unable to live perfect sinless lives, but we are forgiven and made whole through Jesus and His crucifixion.

Paul wrote this to the Christians in Rome, for many were still trying to reconcile the legalism of Judaism with the teachings of Jesus and the teachings of His apostles after His crucifixion. The rules of Judaism at the time were very strict and went far beyond what we see in the Old Testament. Those first Christians in Rome needed to hear this message just as we today need to hear it. Jesus paid the price, and there is no condemnation for those who follow Him.

Additional verses or your thoughts...

Example: How does this verse make you feel?

_____
_____
_____
_____
_____
_____
_____
_____

Bible Verse: Hebrews 8:12 NIV

"For I will forgive their wickedness and will remember their sins no more."

What Does This Mean?

This verse is a reference to the fact that we are all sinners, but it is also a promise that God will not hold our sins against us. God does not make promises that He does not fulfill, and this one is no different. Guilt is not a punishment, for if God does not remember our sins why would He punish us for them? Instead those who hold onto guilt question their worthiness for the love and forgiveness that God promises us.

It is, therefore, your own lack or willingness to forgive that creates a sense of guilt.

Instead of holding onto your own feelings of guilt and/or unworthiness, talk to God about it in prayer and let go. Hold on instead to the promise that He has already forgotten your transgressions, and set an example by forgiving yourself and those around you.

Additional verses or your thoughts...

Example: How does this verse make you feel?

_____
_____
_____
_____
_____

Joy

What is joy? You might have noticed that I separate joy and happiness into two separate emotions to explore. As you think this one through, remember that each generation may have a different definition. It might be helpful to ask some adults that you admire how they define it. For our purposes, I'll lay out a basic answer.

As a noun, joy is the state of happiness and delight. As a verb, it is feeling a strong sensation of pleasure in something.

We are given these feelings for good so that we will prosper and develop strong attachments to our loved ones. It is the pursuit of joy as defined above that can become tricky. Can you think of reasons or places that might be problematic? Let's explore what the Bible says about joy and consider the similarities and the differences.

Bible Verse: Romans 15:13 NIV
"May the God of hope fill you with all joy and peace as you trust in him, so that you may overflow with hope by the power of the Holy Spirit."

What Does This Mean?

This is Paul writing to the Romans. There were so many strong emotions between the Jews and the Romans that finding a space for hope to be seen was powerful. When I read this verse it speaks to me of a happy contentment that goes hand in hand with peace. Intense emotions and feelings of pleasure don't leave much room for peace or hope.

To wrap it up, it is okay to have strong intense emotions, but we aren't expected to live there all the time. Joy as a happy contentment full of peace and hope is a much healthier state of being.

Additional verses or your thoughts...

Example: How does this verse make you feel?

_____
_____
_____
_____
_____
_____
_____
_____
_____
_____
_____
_____
_____
_____
_____
_____
_____

Bible Verse: Psalm 16:11 NIV

""You make known to me the path of life;
  you will fill me with joy in your presence,
  with eternal pleasures at your right hand."

What Does This Mean?

This is a poetic song written by King David. In the verse he makes clear that joy can be an intense happiness, but joy can also be a happy contentment. He also makes it clear that it is good to express the intense emotions in praise to God, but that joy is not all intense pleasure. King David makes the distinction of how worldly pleasures are so easy to come-by, but the joy fills his life is different.

If intensity of emotions is not the definition of joy, then we are free to embrace the intense emotions and also to let them go.

Additional verses or your thoughts…

Example: How does this verse make you feel?

_____
_____
_____
_____
_____
_____
_____
_____
_____
_____

Bible Verse: James 1:2 NIV

"Consider it pure joy, my brothers and sisters, whenever you face trials of many kinds, "

What Does This Mean?

James is talking to those first-century Christians who were experiencing many hardships directly because of their faith in Jesus. For it is not during the good and easy times that our true faith spills out for all to see. That is the testing by fire that is mentioned in Matthew 3:12. For if you have a joyful spirit, a spirit that is happy and content and peaceful, then hardships will refine it.

Yes, you will mourn losses and feel sadness, anger, and all the feelings, but you will come back time and again to peace and contentment.

Writing poetry to express your joy, just like with your anger, sadness, or any other emotion, helps ground you in the positive and let go of the negative.

Additional verses or your thoughts...

Example: How does this verse make you feel?

_____
_____
_____
_____
_____

Happiness

Joy and happiness get separate space because the English language uses them in two different ways. It can be confusing because many people seem to use them as interchangeable words, and in many instances it seems like either word would work. After reading this book you will have a better idea of what the biblical difference is and how to find peace in the differences.

If happiness is not joy, then what is it? Happiness can be defined as a positive state of well-being that cannot be broken down into other positive emotions. The world sees happiness as a feeling that brings a smile to your lips and it is usually paired with an outside stimulus, like good fortune.

What else could happiness be? Consider happiness to be a state where your emotions, your soul, and your mind all meet. Let's explore this thought through a Bible verse.

Bible Verse: Psalm 68:3 NIV
"But may the righteous be glad and rejoice before God; may they be happy and joyful."

What Does This Mean?

Psalms are poetry written for man, but I still think we can glean much from it. For example, the use of happy and joyful suggests that these are understood as separate states of being. God wants good things for us; He wants us to understand in our deepest parts and our minds and for us to express these things in outward ways. As the verse says, rejoice. Do so with both happiness and joy!

Additional verses or your thoughts...

Example: How does this verse make you feel?

Bible Verse: Psalm 118:24 NIV

"The Lord has done it this very day; let us rejoice today and be glad."

What Does This Mean?

This is yet another verse often taken out of context. It is used to encourage us to be joyful and happy everyday, no matter our circumstances. To sing out and rejoice daily, impling that anything less is being ungrateful. Yet, if you read the verse in context, it was written to remind the Jewish people that even during times of great hardship, God was with them and that there is something to be happy about. God walked with them through leaving Egypt and 40 years in the desert. He was there when they crucified Jesus, and through that act, God is with all of us.

Instead of seeing this verse as a reprimand when you are not feeling happy and joyful, use it as a reminder of the blessings God has given you.

So this verse isn't so much proving what the Bible has to say about being happy as much as a reminder to praise God and find happiness in what He has given you. Writing poetry about happiness might not take place while you are feeling happy, but recognizing what you feel like when you are happy is an important step in finding your happiness.

Additional verses or your thoughts...

Example: How does this verse make you feel?

Bible Verse: James 5:13 NIV

"Is anyone among you in trouble? Let them pray. Is anyone happy? Let them sing songs of praise."

What Does This Mean?

James is talking about faith and prayer in this chapter. If you read the whole chapter, you come to see that happiness is just a small part of what he has to say. Taken out of context, this verse is used to encourage singing songs of praise during moments of happiness, and there is nothing wrong with that. However, this verse is talking about so much more than just "sing when you're happy." This verse is talking about having a relationship with God. It is talking about a faith that takes all things to God, the bad and the good. Often we forget the good and only talk to God during the hard parts.

So here is your reminder: talk to God when you are happy, pray, sing, and give thanks. Write a few of your own poems. Have a relationship with God, your father.

Additional verses or your thoughts...

Example: How does this verse make you feel?

_____

_____

_____

_____

_____

_____

HAIKU- REFER TO PAGE 8

5
7
5

5
7
5

5
7
5

HAIKU- REFER TO PAGE 8

5
7
5

5
7
5

5
7
5

HAIKU- REFER TO PAGE 8

5
7
5

5
7
5

5
7
5

CINQUAIN - REFER TO PAGE 10

_____
_____
2 _____
4 _____
6 _____
8 _____
2 _____

_____
_____
2 _____
4 _____
6 _____
8 _____
2 _____

_____
_____
2 _____
4 _____
6 _____
8 _____
2 _____

CINQUAIN- REFER TO PAGE 10

---

2 _____
4 _____
6 _____
8 _____
2 _____

---

2 _____
4 _____
6 _____
8 _____
2 _____

---

2 _____
4 _____
6 _____
8 _____
2 _____

CINQUAIN- REFER TO PAGE 10

_____
_____
2 _____
4 _____
6 _____
8 _____
2 _____

_____
_____
2 _____
4 _____
6 _____
8 _____
2 _____

_____
_____
2 _____
4 _____
6 _____
8 _____
2 _____

FREE FORM- REFER TO PAGE 12

FREE FORM- REFER TO PAGE 12

FREE FORM- REFER TO PAGE 12

FREE FORM- REFER TO PAGE 12

FREE FORM- REFER TO PAGE 12

FREE FORM- REFER TO PAGE 12

FREE FORM- REFER TO PAGE 12

FREE FORM- REFER TO PAGE 12

BLANK VERSE- REFER TO PAGE 14

BLANK VERSE- REFER TO PAGE 14

BLANK VERSE - REFER TO PAGE 14

BLANK VERSE- REFER TO PAGE 14

LIMERICK - REFER TO PAGE 16

```
_____
_____
A _____
A _____
B _____
B _____
A _____
```

```
_____
_____
A _____
A _____
B _____
B _____
A _____
```

```
_____
_____
A _____
A _____
B _____
B _____
A _____
```

LIMERICK - REFER TO PAGE 16

LIMERICK - REFER TO PAGE 16

_____
_____
A _____
A _____
B _____
B _____
A _____

_____
_____
A _____
A _____
B _____
B _____
A _____

_____
_____
A _____
A _____
B _____
B _____
A _____

CLERIHEW- REFER TO PAGE 18

A
A
B
B

A
A
B
B

A
A
B
B

A
A
B
B

CLERIHEW- REFER TO PAGE 18

A
A
B
B

A
A
B
B

A
A
B
B

A
A
B
B

CLERIHEW- REFER TO PAGE 18

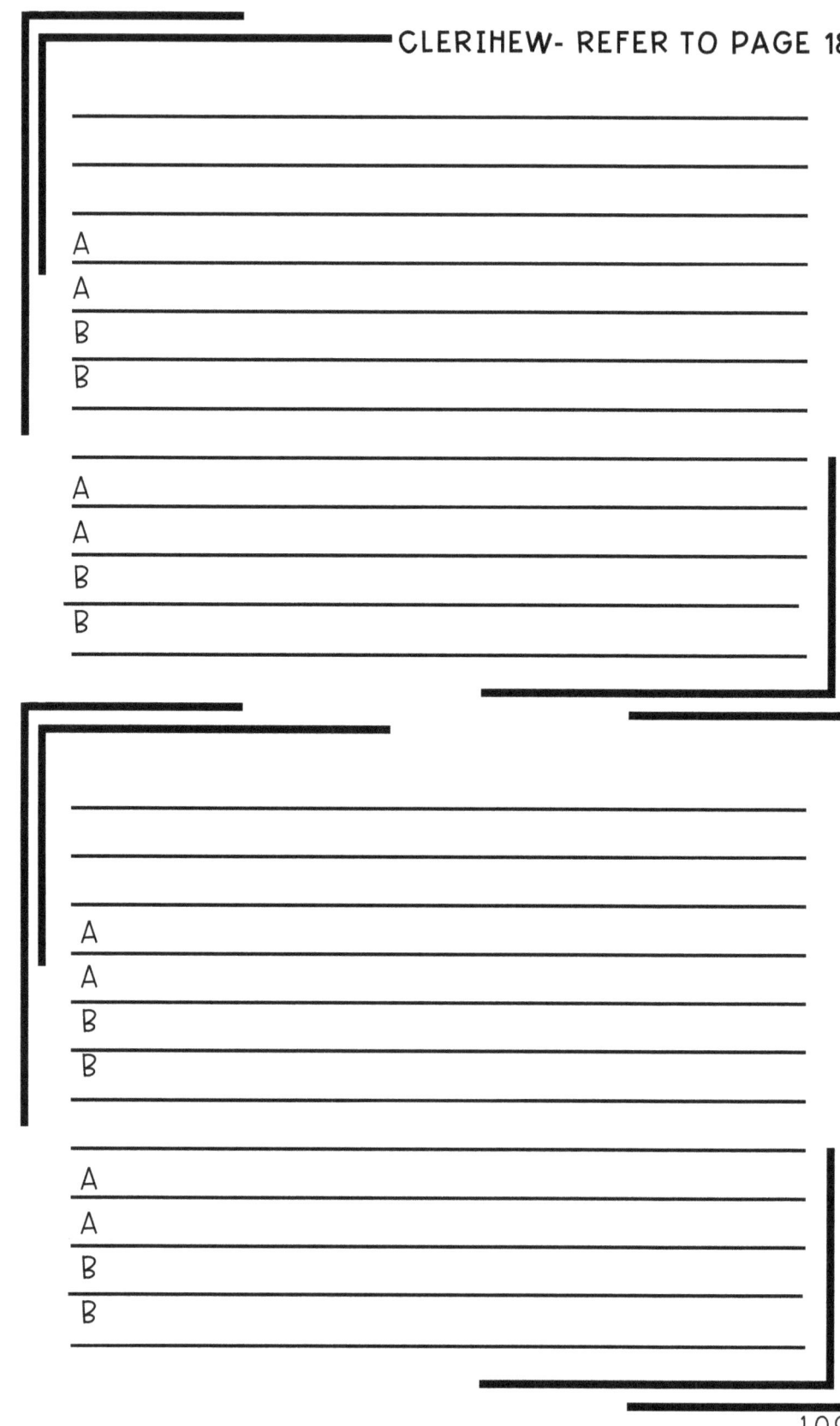

CLERIHEW- REFER TO PAGE 18

A
A
B
B

A
A
B
B

A
A
B
B

A
A
B
B

TRIOLET-REFER TO PAGE 20

_____
_____
_____
_____
1 _____
2 _____
3 _____
4 _____
5 _____
6 _____
7 _____
8 _____

_____
_____
_____
_____
1 _____
2 _____
3 _____
4 _____
5 _____
6 _____
7 _____
8 _____

TRIOLET-REFER TO PAGE 20

1
2
3
4
5
6
7
8

1
2
3
4
5
6
7
8

TRIOLET-REFER TO PAGE 20

1
2
3
4
5
6
7
8

1
2
3
4
5
6
7
8

TRIOLET-REFER TO PAGE 20

1.
2.
3.
4.
5.
6.
7.
8.

1.
2.
3.
4.
5.
6.
7.
8.

DIZAIN - REFER TO PAGE 22

A
B
A
B
B
C
C
D
C
D

A
B
A
B
B
C
C
D
C
D

DIZAIN - REFER TO PAGE 22

A
B
A
B
B
C
C
D
C
D

A
B
A
B
B
C
C
D
C
D

DIZAIN - REFER TO PAGE 22

```
_____
_____
A _____
B _____
A _____
B _____
B _____
C _____
C _____
D _____
C _____
D _____


_____
_____
A _____
B _____
A _____
B _____
B _____
C _____
C _____
D _____
C _____
D _____
```

DIZAIN -REFER TO PAGE 22

A
B
A
B
B
C
C
D
C
D

A
B
A
B
B
C
C
D
C
D

www.ingramcontent.com/pod-product-compliance
Lightning Source LLC
Chambersburg PA
CBHW061809070526
44586CB00024B/2772